Replacing Bad Habits

Discovering SELF Series:

Replacing Bad Habits
(Book Three)

by

Dr. Antwion M. Yowe

Townsend Press
Nashville, Tennessee

Copyright © 2016 Townsend Press

(A division of the Sunday School Publishing Board, NBC, USA, Inc.)

All rights reserved.

No part of this book may be reproduced or transmitted in any form, by any means, electronic or mechanical, including photocopying, recording, or by any information storage or retrieval system without the expressed permission in writing from the publisher. Permission requests may be addressed to Townsend Press, 330 Charlotte Avenue, Nashville, Tennessee 37201-1188; or e-mailed to customercare@sspbnbc.com.

ISBN: 978-1-939225-30-6

Unless otherwise noted, Scripture taken from the Holy Bible, NEW INTERNATIONAL VERSION®, NIV® Copyright © 1973, 1978, 1984, 2011 by Biblica, Inc.® Used by permission. All rights reserved worldwide.

Those marked NKJV are taken from the New King James Version®. Copyright © 1982 by Thomas Nelson. Used by permission. All rights reserved.

Printed in the United States of America

25 24 23 22 21 20 19 18 17 16 – 10 9 8 7 6 5 4 3 2 1

Contents

Foreword vii

Chapter Summary ix

Introduction 1

Chapter

1. Getting Rid of Bad Habits 3
2. Futile Thinking 7
3. Hard Hearts 12
4. How to Counteract Futile Thinking 16
5. Live a Life of Love 20
6. Old Self versus New Self 26
7. Imitators of God 32
8. Making the Most of Every Opportunity 39

Foreword

Replacing Bad Habits is the third book in a four-part intergenerational Bible study series designed to strengthen the core of the twenty-first-century Christian by compelling individuals and families to return to their kitchen tables for sharing, reflection, and learning who they are as part of the body of Christ.

Dr. Yowe's first two books in the Discovering SELF Series—*"Who Am I?"* and *Developing Me*—fully engage the reader and Bible study participant to explore themselves and discover how they are called of God to respond to the issues of life. These offerings were designed to assist the reader in rediscovering their God-given purpose and their value in life as children of God with sacred worth.

Replacing Bad Habits promises to be an experiential encounter with God. In this book, readers are challenged to examine the basis of the choices they make in light of the Word of God. Next, the reader is compelled to replace undesirable choices and behaviors with behaviors and choices that are pleasing in the sight of God.

Bad habits are developed over time, especially when they are not challenged and held to a higher spiritual standard. Just as bad habits are developed, so are habits that are pleasing to God. Replacing bad behavior and habits is a choice that we all must make. Make the right choice, make choices that are based on the Word of God, and realize a greater quality of life.

God promises us His kingdom on earth as it is in heaven. Many Christians are having trouble finding this earthly kingdom and quality of life because they fail to make choices that are consistent with God's will for their lives. Social media, social networking, and the ever-present temptations of life have created pressures too great for the average Christian to bear. Spiritual maturity is at an all-time low, and church relationships leave a lot to be desired in this the twenty-first century.

Dr. Yowe is committed to encouraging Christians to change their worldview of social entertainment to that of spiritual enlightenment. The promises of God are not impossible to attain; realizing them in our lives just takes practice. We hope you consider your bad habits and seek to replace them with habits grounded in the Word of God.

—Dr. Donnell J. Moore
Church Physicians Consulting

Chapter Summary

Chapter 1: Getting Rid of Bad Habits
This chapter identifies and defines what bad habits are and how they are developed. From this understanding, readers are challenged to break bad habits by replacing them with habits that are consistent with God's will for their lives.

Chapter 2: Futile Thinking
Futile thinking is thinking without a purpose, thinking that will not produce a desired outcome or end. In many ways, futile thinking is foolishness and inconsistent with the will of God, who calls us to be sober-minded. In this chapter, we uncover what happens to Christians who use futile thinking to lead and guide their lives.

Chapter 3: Hard Hearts
A hard heart is a heart that is no longer sensitive to the promptings of the Holy Spirit and has no desire to change for the sake of the Gospel of Jesus Christ. When our hearts become hard, we are insensitive to one another, we fail to love, and we are unable to detect when our lives are in danger of falling out of fellowship with God. In this chapter, we discuss how to avoid the hard-heart syndrome.

Chapter 4: How to Counteract Futile Thinking
Futile thinking does not produce a desired outcome. The way to counteract futile thinking is by imitating the truth and being sober-minded. In this chapter, we are challenged to put on the mind of Christ Jesus and to live a life consistent with the way that Jesus lived. The more we live like Jesus, the easier it is to counteract futile thinking.

Chapter 5: Live a Life of Love
Just as bad thinking can be counteracted by living like Jesus lived, bad behaviors can be counteracted by living a life of love—the kind of love that God showed by giving us Jesus, and the kind of love that Jesus showed by dying that we may have life. When our hearts are filled with love, there is no room for bad thinking or behavior.

Chapter 6: Old Self versus New Self
In this chapter, the readers will be exposed to both their old and new natures, and their old and new selves. The old nature or self is based on a life lived outside of salvation. The new self is a life lived after accepting Christ as one's personal Savior. Both selves are important, and we must recognize the sacrifice that Jesus made so that our new selves can be pleasing unto God.

Chapter 7: Imitators of God
In God we have a role model who is the best of the best. As we imitate Him, we are able to exchange bad choices and behaviors with good choices and behaviors. In today's society, we imitate a number of persons who influence our choices, our behaviors, and our lives. Not all of the people we imitate cause us to be pleasing in the sight of God; therefore, we are encouraged to imitate God.

Chapter 8: Making the Most of Every Opportunity
Life is full of challenges and situations that we cannot avoid. We are reminded that although we are Christians we live in an evil world. Since we are constantly challenged by the vicissitudes of life, we are admonished to make the best of every situation and every opportunity that we are given. Not only are we to make good decisions and exhibit good behavior, we are also called to live like Jesus and imitate God. This mandate is possible only when we learn to replace bad habits.

Introduction

"Watch your life and doctrine closely. Persevere in them, because if you do, you will save both yourself and your hearers."
(1 Timothy 4:16)

When I was a child, my grandmother and primary guardian poured the Word of God into my mind, body, and soul daily. However, as a young person struggling to find his way in the world, I was resistant at times. Still, they were persistent and stayed the course, adhering to Proverbs 22:6: "Start children off on the way they should go, and even when they are old they will not turn from it."

During my teenage years, I began to look toward worldly things in hopes of finding a self-made identity. To fit in with my friends and peers, I began to indulge in fleshly vices. I could hear a little voice (my conscience) telling me that the things I was doing were wrong. Yet, I chose to ignore the voice. Gradually, the voice grew fainter and fainter. But, praise God, one day the little voice got louder and louder. I tuned in to it and was kept out of harm's way.

As I look back over my life's journey, I have come to the realization that application of the Word of God and proper training and development of the conscience are among the great keys to self-improvement and truly discovering self.

Thus, the focus of the four-part Discovering SELF series is to help today's Christians become strengthened and equipped in the Word of God, taking the time to study to show themselves approved unto God (see 2 Timothy 2:15). The first two books in the series focused on understanding oneself (identity) and how a person's self is developed.

This third book in the series focuses on replacing bad choices with choices that are based on the Word of God—for it is not enough to merely stop a bad behavior; one must replace that behavior with actions that are pleasing and acceptable to God. The apostle Paul understood this. It is easy to get pulled back into old bad habits.

That is why Paul wrote to the new Christian believers in Ephesus, urging them to stay alert and to "live a life worthy of the calling" they had received.

Like the other books in the Discovering SELF series, *Replacing Bad Habits* has been designed in workbook format to encourage readers to meditate on the Word of God introspectively so that they might discover and develop their true identities as believers. In addition to being prompted to think critically and reflectively, readers are urged to record their thoughts and truths in the space provided. It is hoped that each reader will read, apply, and uncover precious gems that will enhance his or her spiritual journey.

CHAPTER 1

GETTING RID OF BAD HABITS

Getting rid of bad habits may be difficult; however, it is an essential part of our Christian growth and an important step to improving self. *Webster's Dictionary* defines a *habit* as "a pattern of behavior acquired as a result of frequent repetition." So habits, whether good or bad, become ingrained in whom we are as individuals. They are the things we do by second nature without really thinking about them.

When habits are identified as flaws or defects in our Christian personality, it must be our desire to get rid of them. Of course this is much easier said than done; just ask many lifelong smokers. However, if we truly desire spiritual growth and wish to improve ourselves, we must be willing to put in the work to accomplish it.

Rarely is it enough simply to quit practicing bad habits. Remember, habits become a part of who we are. So when we remove a habit we are often left with a void, an empty space in our lives. To fill that void we must replace the negative and bad with the positive and good.

Think again about a smoker trying to kick the habit. Former smokers sometimes replace cigarettes with gum, nicotine patches, or even faux cigarettes to fill the void. Cessation programs for smokers often recommend alternative activities to help smokers break free. The point is, if we truly want to get rid of bad habits we must replace them with good habits.

This is why repentance is often difficult for many Christians. Repentance is to intentionally turn and go in the opposite direction.

Going in the opposite direction means to stop doing what is not pleasing and to begin doing what is acceptable and pleasing unto God. Many Christians have wrongly learned that stopping a bad behavior will make them better. Only when we replace the bad behavior with acceptable behavior will our lives change and become transformed.

The apostle Paul understood how easy it is to get sucked in by old bad habits. That was one of the reasons why, while in prison, he wrote a letter to the church in Ephesus. The believers in Ephesus were like his own children. He had watched the church grow from infancy, assisted them as they struggled to find their identity, and helped them to develop into mature Christians.

We might compare Paul to a parent watching his child go off to college or out into the world. Through the years, the parent lovingly teaches and shapes the child to give that child a good foundation to grow into a mature and independent person. Still, it is with great trepidation that the parent sends the child out into the world, knowing the dangers and negative influences that could impact him or her.

Similarly, Paul was concerned because he knew the world in which the Ephesian Christians lived. The city of Ephesus was known not only for its great wealth and commerce but also for its sexual vices, blood thirst, pagan worship, and practices of black magic and sorcery.

Ephesus was home to what has been regarded as one of the seven wonders of the ancient world—the Temple of Artemis. The temple, though beautifully crafted and architecturally ingenious for that time, promoted idolatrous worship of the Grecian goddess for whom it was named. It was a focal attraction for both residents and tourists, and naturally a dangerous influence for Christians in that city.

Additionally, Ephesus housed an impressive stadium wherein audiences reveled in the bloody gladiator sports hosted there. The city was wholly immoral and rife with sexual innuendos and blatant perversions. Developing the bad habits of following these socially acceptable norms posed a threat to Christian growth in the early church in Ephesus.

There was even more reason for worry; Paul was aware of the city's "dark side." The citizens of Ephesus more than dabbled in sorcery and black magic. Archeological findings indicate that the lives of the Ephesians were greatly influenced by superstitions, omens, and divination. When Paul began evangelizing in Ephesus, he encountered many who eventually became believers who had once practiced the black arts.

Naturally, then, Paul was concerned that some of their old habits might creep back into their young Christian lives. For this reason, Paul wrote a letter to the Ephesian church and urged them to "live a life worthy of the calling [they had] received" (Ephesians 4:1). Like a parent who worries over his young-adult child, Paul did not want the believers to assimilate into the world around them and be consumed once more by the Ephesian lifestyle. He did not want bad habits to rob them of the new life that they received by grace.

Paul's letter to the church in Ephesus is helpful to the Christian who desires to live according to the will of God. In this book, we will examine how we can use Paul's advice to replace bad habits and thereby improve ourselves.

❖ Study Questions

1. Define "habit."

_____
_____
_____

2. Is it enough simply to stop practicing a bad habit? Explain.

_____
_____
_____

3. What is the relationship between the concepts of repentance and transformation?
   _____
   _____
   _____

4. List some of the elements that existed in ancient Ephesus that may have had a negative influence on Christians living in that city.
   _____
   _____
   _____

5. Compare the elements existing in ancient Ephesus with that of the world today.
   _____
   _____
   _____

6. How can Paul's letter to the church in Ephesus help the contemporary Christian?
   _____
   _____
   _____

CHAPTER 2

FUTILE THINKING

So I tell you this, and insist on it in the Lord, that you must no longer live as the Gentiles do, in the futility of their thinking. They are darkened in their understanding and separated from the life of God because of the ignorance that is in them due to the hardening of their hearts. (Ephesians 4:17-18)

Very much of who we are and what we do is based upon the way we think and what we believe. This is proved in both complex and even basic decisions. For example, when we make a simple decision to take an umbrella when we go out, we base that choice on the fact that we believe or think it will rain. More complexly, we may choose to be honest persons because we believe in God, value fairness, and have an established moral code (shaped by the way we think). Our beliefs and thoughts, then, play a large role in the habits that we develop. This is important to understand, because if we can determine what factors drive our habits, we can identify the root cause of those habits we wish to replace.

In Ephesians 4:17-18, Paul isolated a root factor that affected the habits and patterns of the people in Ephesus: the "futility of their thinking." What did Paul mean by that?

Ephesus belonged to the Grecian world, and Greeks were known for their great thinkers. These philosophers were revered as great intellectuals. They sat around and discussed the origin and purpose of life, love, truth, the source of happiness, and so on. Different schools of philosophies held as many different opinions, but it was their ideas that shaped the thinking of the Grecian world.

To get a brief overview and understanding of some of the philosophical ideas of that time, consider the following groups of Greek philosophers:

- **Stoics:** Promoted reason and logic, while ignoring the idea that God was a person. Instead, they viewed God as some force of nature to which the human soul was connected.

- **Epicureans:** Believed in God but did not believe that He was interested in human affairs. They felt that the ultimate source of happiness was pleasure and self-gratification.

- **Cynics:** Believed that pleasure seeking was the ultimate evil and that seeking virtue was the only good in life.

- **Sophists:** Believed that truth and good, right and wrong, was a matter of personal opinion or to be determined by popular culture.

- **Skeptics:** Believed that nothing in life really matters at all.

Although many of the views were in direct conflict with one another, the Greeks considered themselves to be the intellectuals of the ancient world. Their opinions, speculations, and ideas shaped the thinking and habits of popular culture, and as such should be held responsible for the moral decadence of that era. Their philosophies did little to encourage their listeners to seek a lifestyle that was in line with the will of God.

For this reason, Paul regarded their thinking as futile. Other terms used for the word *futile* might be *empty, idle, vain, foolish, purposeless,* or *frustrating*. It is no wonder that Paul used this word to describe the conflicting and confusing theories of the Greek philosophers. Their ideas did not give the people purpose, and for the most part they were based on empty speculation. Yet we can see how a person attempting to follow their logic could be led into a lifestyle separate from God.

Paul stated that these Gentiles were "darkened in their understanding." Instead of these intellectuals enlightening their adherers, they were actually doing the opposite. Their mixed messages gave the people no real guidance, nor a true sense of right and wrong. As a result, immorality was rampant. People did whatever they wanted, with no holy fear of the Lord.

The apostle went on to state that the city of Ephesus was separated from the life of God because of their ignorance. Paul was by no means calling these philosophers dummies. Rather, he was referring to their deliberate choice to remain ignorant of God and His will. In another letter, Paul referred to a people who "knew God" but who "neither glorified him as God nor gave thanks to him, but their thinking became futile" (Romans 1:21). It was inconvenient to their lifestyle to worship the Lord, and so they chose to remain ignorant of Him.

Paul warned the believers in ancient Ephesus not to live like the people in the world around them. That same counsel is applicable to us today. We live in a world full of great thinkers. We must be careful, though, because not all thoughts are productive.

Internet search engines and the like have replaced the schools of philosophy. The world is full of information. Often the information is conflicting and even downright inaccurate. If this is what we are feeding our minds, then this is what is shaping our habits. If we expect to change our bad habits, then we will need to change our way of thinking. The Bible admonishes us to seek first God's kingdom. This suggests that we must be careful to know more of the Word than we know of other disciplines of knowledge. It is good to have book knowledge, and it is good to have degrees of higher learning; however, none of these are helpful if our quest for knowledge is not based first on acquiring knowledge of the love of God that is found in Christ Jesus. Too many good Christians have been led astray because they were more interested in the things of the world, and neglected to gain knowledge of what "thus says the Lord." Learning more of God and His Word will change the way you think.

❖ Study Questions

1. Explain how our beliefs and thoughts are related to our habits.

2. Why is it important to understand the factors that drive our habits?

3. What root factor affected the habits and behaviors of the ancient Grecian world?

4. How do the schools of philosophy mentioned earlier contrast with the will of God?

5. Why is the term "futile" appropriate when referring to worldly wisdom?

6. What did the apostle Paul mean when he said the people of Ephesus were "darkened in their understanding and separated from the life of God because of the ignorance that is in them"?

7. In today's world, why must we be cautious of some mediums of information?

_____

_____

_____

8. On what should our quest for knowledge be based?

_____

_____

_____

CHAPTER 3

HARD HEARTS

They are darkened in their understanding and separated from the life of God because of the ignorance that is in them due to the hardening of their hearts. Having lost all sensitivity, they have given themselves over to sensuality so as to indulge in every kind of impurity, and they are full of greed. (Ephesians 4:18-19)

In the Bible, the word *conscience* is rarely used. More often it is alluded to by the word *heart*. The heart in the context of Scripture represents our inner person—the thoughts, values, morals, and perceptions that cause us to act the way we do. The condition of our hearts or consciences directly impacts the habits that we form.

When talking about the world of unbelievers, Paul said that their hearts had become hardened. He used a word picture to emphasize just how desensitized the people had become. Here is an illustration: if you do not often engage in manual labor you may have nicely manicured, soft hands. Thus, when you first go out to rake leaves in your yard, your hands may be sensitive and the rake will likely feel abrasive and uncomfortable. However, if you rake long enough, calluses will begin to form on your hands. While unpleasant to look at, the calluses block the sensation of the rake's irritation. In other words, the tender skin no longer feels the irritation or pain associated with coming in contact with the abrasive elements.

Paul said that this is what had happened to the hearts of the unbelieving Ephesians. The continued exposure to abrasive elements—the empty philosophical thinking and immoral behavior—had caused their hearts to become callused to the point that they felt no remorse or shame over the way they lived. According to many of the philosophers of their day, they had no reason to be regretful because God either did not exist or did not care. They pointed instead to self-pleasure and self-governance.

As a result, the people's consciences no longer stung them when they did wrong. They had "lost all sensitivity." In other words, they felt no pain when they sinned against God. They continued to do wrong over and over again, and that repetition led to the emergence of bad habits. Today, we witness this same level of callousness. We have abused God's grace to the point that if we are not immediately "zapped" or reprimanded for the wrongs that we do, eventually we become insensitive to our wrongs and unwelcomed behavior and they in turn become a way of life.

The Scripture states that the Ephesians gave themselves over, indicating that they willfully and deliberately sold their souls to pleasure and the devil's work. It is sad to contemplate, because this shows that they not only gave themselves over but also *gave up on themselves*. The idea of living with no moral code simply because "you only live once" is the expression of an individual who is without hope for the future.

Paul stated that because of their desensitized condition, the unbelievers proceeded to engage in all sorts of unholy conduct. Their appetites for the immoral proved to be insatiable. Paul said that they had "a continual lust for more." This indicates that the behavior was repetitive and habit-forming. Their psyche became wired to this code of conduct, and it would take a lot of effort and undoing to break free of these bad habits and replace them with good ones.

In today's climate in which almost anything goes, people of God have an intense struggle to protect their hearts from becoming desensitized to their inherent sense of right and wrong. The media promote a carefree, "answer-to-none" ethic through movies and television sitcoms. Many video games and simulations glorify sex, drugs, and crime. Celebrities and star athletes are idolized, even though many of them are the very opposite of what a true role model should be due to their indulgence in immoral and criminal activities. Politicians and even some religious leaders either openly support or passively condone lifestyles that are contradictory to the way that God intends for us to live.

Thus, the believing Christian must work hard to keep her or his conscience properly aligned with God's Word. To do otherwise would spell disaster. As Paul indicated, when you open the door for bad habits to creep in, you will find yourself "given over" and consumed by a continual lust for more. Believers must therefore be on guard to protect their hearts from becoming hardened like that of the unbelieving Ephesians.

❖ Study Questions

1. What does the word *heart* usually mean when found in biblical texts?

   _____
   _____
   _____

2. How is it that the hearts of the ancient Ephesians became hardened?

   _____
   _____
   _____

3. Paul stated that the unbelievers of Ephesus had "given themselves over." What similar pattern do we witness in today's society?

   _____
   _____
   _____

4. List features of modern culture that often expose unwary Christians to the risk of becoming desensitized to God's standard of good and evil.

5. In order to counteract negative influences that would cause the Christian heart to become hardened, what must believers endeavor to do?

CHAPTER **4**

HOW TO COUNTERACT FUTILE THINKING

That, however, is not the way of life you learned when you heard about Christ and were taught in him in accordance with the truth that is in Jesus. (Ephesians 4:20-21)

Therefore do not be foolish, but understand what the Lord's will is. (Ephesians 5:17)

In chapter 2 of this study, it was established that misinformation and baseless ideology have a negative impact on our behavior and habits. It is then the task of believers to counteract thoughts that are deemed as useless, foolish, and futile. Simply put, we must replace bad (useless) knowledge with good (useful) knowledge. But, really, what is good knowledge? Where can we get it? And how will it affect our habits?

The apostle Paul did not leave us in the dark. When talking to the church in Ephesus, he reminded them of the knowledge that they should have been seeking—that is, the knowledge of Christ. Paul was talking to them about more than a superficial knowledge of who Christ is. In fact, this was the trouble among some of the believers; they possessed only a surface knowledge of Christ. Earlier, Paul compared such ones to a sea vessel "blown here and there by every wind of teaching and by the cunning and craftiness of people in their deceitful scheming" (Ephesians 4:14b).

Paul urged Christians to reflect on the things they had heard about Christ, and the things that Paul had personally taught them. Paul's words in the phrase "you . . . were taught in him in accordance with the truth" imply more than just hearing about Jesus. Rather, it implies a process of studying a subject, like in a school.

Paul went on to say that the "truth . . . is in Jesus." We know this to be accurate because Jesus Himself said, "I am the way and the truth and the life" (John 14:6a). So then, good knowledge—truthful knowledge—is directly linked to Jesus. It is thus imperative that believers come to know Christ. Much of this would include a study of Jesus' life and ministry as a man on earth. An intimate study of the Gospels reveals that Jesus lived the truth. How appropriate, then, it is for a Christian desiring to replace bad habits to study and imitate the example left by our Lord Jesus.

Another important part of knowing Christ is accepting Him as our Savior. Understanding the value of His blood and what it has done for us is a humbling concept. When we reflect on how He bore the cross for our sins, we come to learn the love that He has for each of us. That love is empowering! With the love of Christ we are able to accomplish all things, including ridding ourselves of bad habits.

In addition, Paul stated that all believers must have knowledge of what God's will is. He prefaced his statement with this admonition: "do not be foolish." Again, recall the philosophy of that day—God does not exist, God does not care, and truth is relative. Paul knew all of this ideology to be foolishness, futile thinking, and he did not want to see the Ephesian Christians get caught up in these spurious teachings.

For this reason, Paul told the church to "understand what the Lord's will is." In an earlier verse, Paul said to "find out what pleases the Lord." God has given us His holy Word—the Old and the New Testaments. By reading and studying it, we can come to understand His will for us. We can learn the behaviors that are pleasing to the Lord, and the ones that are not. "For everything that was written in the past was written to teach us, so that through the endurance taught in the Scriptures and the encouragement they provide we might have hope" (Romans 15:4).

By increasing our knowledge of God's Word, we are able to replace useless knowledge with useful knowledge. That knowledge is key to transforming our lives, by getting rid of bad habits and replacing them with habits that are good and pleasing to our God.

In summation, we learned that to replace bad habits we must replace bad knowledge. Greek philosophy was bad knowledge. In the two verses highlighted at the outset of this chapter, Paul successfully disputed some of their most popular theories:

- God does exist; therefore, believers are to take time to come to know Him.
- God does care, because He has a will that Christians must come to understand.
- Truth is not relative, but it is in Jesus. When we learn the Christ we find truth.
- How we live does matter. We are Christians, followers of Christ.

Why does it matter to us today that Paul disputed those philosophies? Whether we realize it for what it is or not, those theories have subtle undercurrents in today's world, even in areas where religion is prominent. The world in general lives as if God does not exist or does not care how people choose to live. Many live by the standard that "you only live once, so do whatever pleases you regardless of how it may impact or influence others." If we do not make a conscious effort, we may find ourselves drawn along by this ideology. By choosing not to accept the misinformation that the world is feeding you, but instead taking the time and effort to search for truth, you will be able to successfully improve self by replacing bad habits and building a good reputation with both God and others.

❖ Study Questions

1. What must we do to counteract futile thinking?

_____
_____
_____

2. What happens when individuals settle for mere surface knowledge of Christ?
___
___
___

3. Why can it be said that good knowledge is directly linked to Jesus?
___
___
___

4. Besides learning about how Jesus lived, what is another important factor that is imperative to our coming to know the Christ?
___
___
___

5. What unique tool helps us to "understand what the Lord's will is"?
___
___
___

6. How did Paul use his knowledge of Scripture to dispute the popular theories of philosophy of his day?
___
___
___

CHAPTER 5

LIVE A LIFE OF LOVE

[Live a life of love], just as Christ loved us and gave himself up for us as a fragrant offering and sacrifice to God. (Ephesians 5:2)

In the previous chapter, we discussed how to counteract bad thinking. Now we will discuss how to counteract bad behaviors formed as a result of a hardened or calloused conscience. Remember, in his letter to the church in Ephesus, Paul stated that many had "given themselves over" to a life of self-indulgence and moral depravity. Now Paul was counseling the Christians not to follow in that path. Instead, he urged them to "live a life of love." What did he mean?

We understand that love is a positive and powerful emotion. With it in our hearts we have little room for negativity; and because it is emotive, we lower the risk of becoming desensitized by the cold and callous world around us. To better understand how love works, we should first understand what love is and what it is not.

In a letter to another church Paul defined *love*. A careful study of 1 Corinthians 13:4-8 reveals much about this quality, and will help us to learn what it means to "live a life of love." The following table gives a brief overview of those verses.

What Love Is	What Love Is Not
Patient	Envious
Kind	Boastful
Rejoice with truth	Delighted with evil

What Love Is	What Love Is Not
Strong	Rude
Trusting	Self-seeking
Hopeful	Easily angered
Persevering	Begrudging

Love is patient. Love helps us to be patient with others and ourselves. Love acknowledges that we are all imperfect and are works in progress. Therefore, this positive quality allows us to patiently accept one another as we work to improve the persons we are to become the persons we desire to be.

Love is kind. Love is proactive. It inspires us to look for ways we can show kindness to others. The kindness of love is manifested both by our encouraging words and benevolent acts to those in need.

Love is joyful with truth. Genuine love is open and honest. It begins with us individually. We must be honest with ourselves about who we are, even when at times the truth may be painful. We must also be honest in our interactions with others. Love is not deceitful or conniving.

Love is strong. The most common rendering for 1 Corinthians 13:7a reads, "[love] bears all things" (NKJV). The word could also be translated as "covers." Either way, the idea being conveyed is that love is not a weak quality but a strong one. Love is strong enough to withstand the shortfalls, mistakes, and sins of others without being broken. Truth is found in the words "love each other deeply, because love covers over a multitude of sins" (1 Peter 4:8).

Love is trusting. Not to be confused, love is not gullible or blissfully naïve. Yet love is neither pessimistic nor always looking for fault. Unless there is a valid reason to do otherwise, a loving person is willing to believe and trust rather than be judgmental and accusatory.

Love is hopeful. Just as love is trusting, love is also hopeful. Love will move a person to hope for the best instead of assume the worst. Love will not allow us to give up on an individual or situation. Love positively looks toward the future and believes in the opportunity that it holds.

Love is persevering. No person is exempt from hard times, whether personal storms or shared struggles and disappointments. When we are battling difficult circumstances, love buoys us. It is love—love from God, love from family and friends, and love of self—that enables us to endure to continue the fight. Love empowers us to be tenacious. It gives us the strength to continue to stay in the ring and keep getting back up no matter how many times we get knocked down.

Love is not envious. Envy is a negative emotion. It makes us unappreciative of what we have been blessed with because we are too busy coveting the blessings of others. Envy is the very opposite of love. It is destructive and divisive. It destroys the person that we have the potential to be, and it disrupts the peace that we should enjoy with others.

Love is not boastful. If we possess the genuine quality of love, we will abound in kindness and noble deeds, but that is no reason to become boastful. Our motivation for our actions should never be to put ourselves in the limelight. Love is not a praise seeker. It does not toot its own horn. Love would never exalt itself to make someone else feel small or unworthy. On the contrary, love looks for ways to lift others.

Love is not delighted with evil. There exist people in this world who revel in the downfall of others, deviously hoping for other people's failure. This is not the way of love. Neither is it love to encourage someone in doing things that you know to be wrong. Love does not condone inappropriate behavior, nor does it take pleasure in the mistakes and troubles of others.

Love is not rude. A person who is rude shows little consideration or regard for others. Such people often speak carelessly without giving any thought to how their words may hurt someone else. A believer who bears the mark of love is cautious of how his or her words might affect others. Rather than act with shocking behavior and loose conduct, they are well-mannered, morally principled, and respectful.

Love is not self-seeking. Love is not selfish. People who are self-centered or egotistical are usually willing to do whatever it takes to get what they want and to make known their importance. They have little concern for those they may hurt in the process. Love, however, is selfless. A loving person is willing to make sacrifices and concessions.

Love is not easily angered. Again, we must acknowledge that none of us is perfect and that we all have our idiosyncrasies. At times we tend to get on one another's nerves, even to the point of angering one another. However, love will not allow us to remain angry. It will encourage us to work on improving our temperament. We may recognize in ourselves a personality flaw of being overly sensitive or easily provoked. With time, hard work, and patience, love can help us to overcome our hair-trigger tempers so that we can co-exist more peacefully with others.

Love is not begrudging. Love is forgiving. Even when we have been treated poorly, love will help us to let go and move on. Love does not keep a tally sheet of all the slights and wrongs that someone has ever done against us. Rather, we remember how all of our sins have been washed away and we have been made clean in Christ's blood. If God can forgive us of all the things we have done both in ignorance and as believers, we must be willing to forgive one another without keeping score.

Therefore, if we endeavor to cultivate the quality of love and all that it means, we will find that we have little room for the negative emotions and behaviors that sear our consciences. In imitation of our God and Savior, we will seek to live lives of love. We will avoid following after the lifestyles promoted by the world, which does not know or acknowledge the Lord. Instead, we will incorporate the principle of love, and thus prove ourselves to be children of God who desire to improve self and reflect God's light.

❖ Study Questions

1. What divine quality is essential to counteracting bad behavior, and how does this quality accomplish that task?

   _____

   _____

   _____

2. Read 1 Thessalonians 5:14. If we are to avoid bad habits by living a life of love, why must we be patient?

   _____

   _____

   _____

3. Why can it be said that love is strong?

   _____

   _____

   _____

4. Read Romans 5:5. How does love help us to remain hopeful?

   _____

   _____

   _____

5. Read 2 Corinthians 4:16. How does love help us even in difficult or negative situations?

   _____

   _____

   _____

6. Read Proverbs 14:30. Explain why love and envy are incompatible.

7. Read 1 Peter 5:5. How does this verse help us to be mindful of boastfulness?

8. Read 1 Corinthians 10:24. What does the phrase "love is not self-seeking" mean?

9. Read Colossians 3:13. How does this principle help us to "live a life of love"?

10. How will cultivating love help us in our quest to counteract negative thoughts, attitudes, and behaviors?

CHAPTER 6

OLD SELF VERSUS NEW SELF

You were taught, with regard to your former way of life, to put off your old self, which is being corrupted by its deceitful desires; to be made new in the attitude of your minds; and to put on the new self, created to be like God in true righteousness and holiness. (Ephesians 4:22-24)

Paul had personally preached Christ to the believers in Ephesus. He was aware of their body of knowledge and knew that the attitudes and conduct of the world around them was not consistent with what they had been taught. So to keep them encouraged and fortified against the devil's works, Paul counseled them to recall the things they had been taught.

Paul refered to an "old self" and a "new self." Commentators generally agree that the apostle was referring to the unconverted person and the saved individual, respectively. So the "old self" refers to the lifestyle led by the unbeliever prior to coming to know the Lord. The "new self" would then be the new life of a person reborn in Christ (see John 3:3).

In his counsel, Paul created a vivid word picture to describe how complete Christian transformation should be. The phrase "to put off" carries the same idea as taking off one's clothes. It represents a complete and deliberate change. Imagine a man that has been invited to a formal affair late in the evening. During the day, he decides to go to the gym for his daily workout. He changes into his gym clothes and sneakers. He enjoys an intense workout and his clothes are saturated with sweat. He checks his watch and observes that he has about an hour or so to finish preparing for the evening event. He packs his things and hurries home. As he gets ready for the evening, would you expect him to rush in and throw on a tuxedo over his gym clothes? Would he take off his shorts and sneakers, but leave on his gym shirt under his dinner jacket? Would he take a shower and then put his sweaty gym clothes back on?

Of course those scenarios are not at all what we would expect of a cultured gentleman. In fact, all of those suggestions seem pretty exaggerated and ridiculous. It is more likely that, after careful grooming and attending to hygiene, the gentleman would don his formal attire and arrive at the event looking neat and manicured, with no traces remaining of the earlier workout. In other words, the gentleman's attire would undergo a complete transformation. He would deliberately remove every article of gym clothing, thoroughly cleanse himself, and purposefully groom with the intention of making a nice appearance for the formal affair.

That is the idea the apostle Paul was trying to convey. The "old person" who had once lived in the Christians of Ephesus had to be completely stripped away. They needed to cleanse themselves of all the bad habits that soiled their reputations and souls. Then they needed to deliberately and purposefully put on a new and better person as a proper response to the grace of God given them in Christ.

In the text, Paul stated that the old person "is being corrupted by its deceitful desires." There are key details that can be learned from this statement. First, the phrase "is being" indicates that the process of corruption is ongoing or continuous. If left unchecked, the "old person" would continue in a downward spiral. We see evidence of this as we view the world collectively. Few would argue that the moral climate of the world has gone from bad to worse, and it continues to spiral out of control.

Second, Paul used the descriptive phrase "deceitful desires." Some texts limit the "desires" mentioned here to those of a sexual nature, and so they translate the word *desires* as "lusts." However, the original Greek word leads us to believe that Paul was referring to much more than carnal pleasures. In fact, Paul was speaking of any type of passion or craving a person may have. This includes ambition, fame, wealth, pleasure, or power, which might all be considered desires of the heart or inner person.

Paul was trying to help his audience to understand that the natural inclination of the inner person is deceptive. Jeremiah 17:9 states that "the heart is deceitful above all things." Many of the things that our hearts naturally long for are destructive. Of course they often do not appear to be that way. Rather, they seem to be appealing and advantageous. They are deceitful. When led by these desires, a person is no longer rational or driven by common sense. Instead, the person is being influenced by the empty promises of happiness and pleasure. But these promises are only illusions crafted by the evil magician, the devil.

In order to conquer wayward desires, wrote Paul in his letter, "be made new in the attitude of your minds." Keeping in mind his context, Paul was speaking to an audience that had already undergone conversion. Why, then, would they still need to be made new? The simple answer is this: old habits die hard. Given the opportunity, former habits may reemerge or new ones may begin to develop.

Consider again the word picture the apostle used. When we remove soiled clothes and put on clean ones, do we expect that our new attire will never get dirty again, that we can wear those same clothes for the rest of our lives? Of course not. Similarly, because we are imperfect, we cannot expect that once we make the transformation from unbeliever to believer that we will never again transgress.

Therefore, it is fitting that Paul would exhort the church to continue to be made new. Like the early Christians in Ephesus, Christians today must coexist among those who lack moral principles or a love for God. We must also deal with our own personal anxieties. Even though we have "put on" the new person, our character is under constant attack. We can be encouraged in knowing that the Lord not only understands and sympathizes with us, but He also gives us what we need to regenerate. In 2 Corinthians 4:16 we are told, "Though outwardly we are wasting away, yet inwardly we are being renewed day by day." Yes, our God gives us the power of renewal with each day that we are given breath. Each day is an opportunity to be made new by His Word and His Spirit.

Ephesians 4:23 reveals where the renewal process must begin; the verse says to make new "the attitude of your minds." The common phrase "Attitude is everything," to a large extent, is true because it is our attitudes—our way of thinking and feeling—that shape our personalities.

In Romans 12:2, Paul put it another way: "be transformed by the renewing of your mind." Paul was recommending that Christians reprogram their mentality. Science has proved that this is possible. The brain transmits information through signals across neurons. As the signal travels, it leaves imprints or memories. The next time the same signal is sent, the nerves recognize and respond more quickly. As this process is repeated again and again, a pattern of thinking is developed. So then, the type of information we feed it can renew the mind.

In both the books of Romans and Ephesians, Paul used verb forms that suggest that this is a continual process. So Christians would continue to renew or refresh the "attitude of [their] mind" by studying God's Word. As they repeatedly take in knowledge and meditate reflectively on what they learn, the brain is reprogrammed to no longer follow fleshly desires. Instead, the individual becomes attuned to the divine will of God. A rejuvenation of the mind leads to a renewal of self. An individual can be declared a new person because that person's thinking, emotions, desires, and actions now reflect God's image. The new person resembles God in "true righteousness and holiness." This image is a stark contrast to the "old person" who indulged in "deceitful desires."

In summation, these verses in the book of Ephesians teach us that we must first recognize that we are innately driven by our fleshly desires and that if we allow them to take control we only spiral downward into moral degradation alienated from God. Second, we can successfully reprogram our minds to follow the Holy Spirit, instead of being led by the flesh, by continuing to study the Bible, meditate on it, and then obey God. Lastly, when we renew our minds, it leads to a change in attitude and a change in self. We become new persons, leaving behind bad habits and reflecting the Lord's righteousness and holiness.

❖ Study Questions

1. To what was Paul referring when he used the terms "old self" and "new self"?

   _____

   _____

   _____

2. How did Paul use a word picture to convey the measure of transformation that must take place in a Christian's life?

   _____

   _____

   _____

3. What results when the unbeliever's lifestyle goes unchecked and is led by the flesh?

   _____

   _____

   _____

4. Is the phrase "deceitful desires" restricted to matters of illicit sexual pleasures? Explain.

   _____

   _____

   _____

5. Why was it necessary for Paul to encourage his already-converted audience "to be made new in the attitude of [their] minds"?

_____
_____
_____

6. After putting on the new person, why must we remain vigilant?

_____
_____
_____

7. Explain how we renew our minds.

_____
_____
_____

CHAPTER 7

IMITATORS OF GOD

[Be imitators of God], therefore, as dearly loved children. (Ephesians 5:1)

A father comes home after a hard day's work and takes off his hat and boots. After taking a shower, he walks into the family room to find his four-year-old son stomping around in his boots and hardhat and a toy tool belt. The father grins and asks, "What are you doing, Michael?" The little boy looks up, with eyes wide and a big smile, and says, "I am you, Daddy! I am going to be just like you when I get big!"

At a young age, Michael knew that his dad was a hard worker. Not only that, he knew him to be loving, kind, and strong, and a family man. Michael admired those qualities, and Daddy was his hero. Michael wanted to imitate the example that his father set.

Some psychologists have declared that copying one's parents is one of the most powerful tools for teaching children. While instruction and discipline are important, a child responds more readily to what he sees parents do than what he hears parents say.

Christians do not find it odd, then, that the apostle Paul would encourage his audience to become imitators of God. Like little Michael, as children of God we desire to be just like our Father. Striving to imitate Him will aid us in our quest to replace bad habits with good habits. In this chapter, we will discuss how imitating God's perfect qualities will help us to improve self.

We know that we cannot perfectly imitate God's qualities, just as four-year-old Michael could never expect to perfectly mimic his father. However, as we prayerfully ask the Lord for His Spirit and humbly study His Word, in time the Holy Spirit will bear fruit within us so that we may improve our reflection of the Father. In Galatians 5:22-23, the godly qualities produced by means of the Holy Spirit are listed.

Fruit of the Holy Spirit
Love
Joy
Peace
Patience
Kindness
Goodness
Faithfulness
Gentleness
Self-control

Love. First John 4:8 tells us that God is love. God's love for us was made manifest when He sent His Son into the world to die for us. There is no love greater than that. Although we could never expect to reflect His love to the perfect degree, we can cultivate the beautiful quality of love. We show that we love God by being obedient to Him. We also imitate Him by loving one another. "If we love one another, God lives in us and his love is made complete in us" (1 John 4:12).

Joy. Joy is the state of being happy. It describes both the feelings of the inner person and the appearance of the outer person. The Bible describes the Lord as a happy God. He rejoices in His works and His faithful people. He delights in seeing others who are likewise happy. Therefore, we imitate Him and bear fruit of the Spirit when we are joyful. We should be especially joyful in our worship. Psalm 100:2 commands us to "worship the LORD with gladness; come before him with joyful songs."

Peace. Peace is another quality of God, listed third among the fruit of the Spirit. Peace is a state of serenity and order. Concerning God, 1 Corinthians 14:33a states this: "For God is not a God of disorder but of peace." The Lord is the source of all peace. In order to enjoy peace we must be in union with the Lord. The Bible says that "there is no peace . . . for the wicked" (Isaiah 48:22). So then, we must endeavor to enter into God's peace by obediently living by His Word. Only then can we expect to receive "the peace of God, which transcends all understanding" (Philippians 4:7).

Patience. *Merriam-Webster Dictionary* has defined *patience* as "the capacity to remain calm and not become annoyed when waiting for a long time or when dealing with problems or difficult people." Indeed, patience is a virtue. Our heavenly Father has demonstrated this beautiful quality time and again when dealing with imperfect humans. Recall the patience that He showed toward the ancient people of Israel. Remember how the Lord demonstrated patience with the disciples who repeatedly argued over who was greatest among them. He did not become angry and disown them. No, He patiently taught them lessons in humility on several occasions. Think of the patience that He shows to each of us. Despite our flaws and imperfections, the Lord patiently waits and shows us how to improve ourselves. He does not become annoyed or give up on us. In a similar way, we must develop the virtue of patience. We must learn to put up with one another without becoming angry or annoyed. We must strive to patiently endure difficult situations without becoming hopeless and giving up.

Kindness. Kindness is a simple principle but, sadly, it is often lacking in today's world. More often, selfishness seems to crowd out opportunities for kindness. Still, there are those who take an active interest in the well-being of others and do not hesitate to perform helpful and friendly favors without being asked. By doing so, they reflect God's kindness. The Lord does not limit His act of kindness to only those who act kindly. Matthew 5:45 reads, "He causes his sun to rise on the evil and the good, and sends rain on the righteous and the unrighteous." So, in imitation of God, we must learn to be kind even to those who may not act kindly toward us.

Goodness. Psalm 25:8a declares that "good and upright is the LORD." Our God is good in the ultimate and absolute sense of the word. There exists no evil intent, injustice, or deceit in Him. Goodness, then, is defined as "moral excellence." It is sincere through and through, with no hint of badness. It is manifested by beneficent acts. Similar to that of kindness, our display of goodness should not be limited toward only others who are also good. When instructing His disciples, Jesus said, "If you do good to those who are good to you, what credit is that to you? Even sinners do that. . . . But love your enemies, do good to them, and lend to them without expecting to get anything back. Then your reward will be great, and you will be children of the Most High, because he is kind to the ungrateful and wicked" (Luke 6:33, 35).

Faithfulness. Throughout the Old and the New Testaments the Lord is declared to be a God that is known for His faithfulness. He is faithful in His promises (see Deuteronomy 7:9 and Hebrews 10:23). He is faithful to deliver His people (see Psalm 25:10; 1 Corinthians 10:13; and 2 Thessalonians 3:3). He is faithful to His own moral code and standards (see Deuteronomy 32:4 and 2 Timothy 2:13).

God is constant and reliable, even to the smallest details. James 1:17b describes Him as one "who does not change like shifting shadows." A shadow changes in size and direction as the day progresses, but God does not change with time. Because He is faithful, we can put our faith in Him. We show ourselves to be faithful by being loyal and constant both to God and with other people. When we give our word, it should be our bond.

We should be reliable and loyal within our friendships. We should not waver on the matters of our moral and ethical principles. In this way, we show that we are imitating God's example of faithfulness. We can be sure that the Lord takes note and rewards all expressions of faithfulness. As believers, then, we must strive to be faithful in all things, no matter how big or small.

Gentleness. Some might consider the quality of gentleness to be an effeminate trait. Others may view it as a sign of weakness in character. However, the fact that the highest personage in the universe displays gentleness is proof that it is neither gender specific nor an inferior quality. One theologian expressed it this way: "There is gentleness in *praus* [Greek word meaning "gentle"], but behind the gentleness there is the strength of steel." Mildness is exercised even in the face of provocation, and therefore requires a balance of reason and restraint.

Mildness is also a quality that draws people. It is endearing. Jesus said of Himself, "Come to me, all you who are weary and burdened, and I will give you rest. Take my yoke upon you and learn from me, for I am gentle and humble in heart, and you will find rest for your souls" (Matthew 11:28-29). As followers of Christ, we desire to imitate His quality of gentleness. Rather than being harsh, abrasive, and unapproachable, we should be gentle, mild-mannered, and amicable.

Self-control. The last of the fruit listed in Galatians 5:23 is self-control. Self-control implies the ability to keep oneself in check or exercise control over one's own actions, speech, and thoughts. Although this quality is possibly one of the most difficult to master, it is a trait that God has shown constantly in His dealings with humans.

Each day, despite our best intentions, we do and say things that fall short of God's glory. We may be guilty of doing things that disappoint or even anger Him. However, He does not act on those emotions. Instead of taking immediate actions against us as wrongdoers, He exercises self-control. He restrains His hand from bringing us to ruin and allows us time to correct ourselves through repentance. Similarly, we should not be quick to judgment and action when we perceive that we may have been slighted. We also show self-control by keeping ourselves in check when fleshly desires try to override the godly standard of right and wrong.

All nine of the aforementioned qualities are essential to developing self. As imitators of God, we strive to manifest these traits in everyday life. By doing so we are able to replace bad habits with good and positive ones.

We need not be disappointed that we cannot perfectly reflect all aspects of the fruit of the Spirit. Rather, we should recognize the need for constant improvement as an opportunity for growth and refinement as we continue to be renewed in the attitudes of our minds.

❖ Study Questions

1. What simple tool have psychologists long thought to be most effective in teaching young children?

   _____
   _____

2. Although we are imperfect, through Bible study, prayer, and the help of the Holy Spirit, what can we hope to achieve?

   _____
   _____

3. How can we imitate our Father in displaying the following qualities?

   a. **Love** (Read 1 John 4:8.)

   _____
   _____

b. **Joy** (Read Proverbs 27:11.)

_____

_____

c. **Peace** (Read John 14:27.)

_____

_____

d. **Patience** (Read 2 Peter 3:9.)

_____

_____

e. **Kindness** (Read Psalm 86:15.)

_____

_____

f. **Goodness** (Read Psalm 100:5.)

_____

_____

g. **Faithfulness** (Read 1 Corinthians 10:13.)

_____

_____

h. **Self-control** (Read Psalm 78:38.)

_____

_____

CHAPTER 8

MAKING THE MOST OF EVERY OPPORTUNITY

Be very careful, then, how you live—not as unwise but as wise, making the most of every opportunity, because the days are evil. (Ephesians 5:15-16)

Most people would agree that life is a busy occupation. No matter what time of year or what season, we always seem to find that we are busy with things to do and little time left in between. Oftentimes people become so caught up in their activities that they give little thought to self-improvement or their spirituality. Those who do may procrastinate or make promises that are never realized. They may feel that there is simply not enough time for them to accomplish everything.

While it is understandable that we must fulfill certain obligations and that certain priorities occupy a lot of our time, we as Christians must be careful to allot time to work on ourselves and our spiritual health; this should be a high priority. It helps if we can first appreciate three key principles about time.

- **Time is precious.** Time is a rare commodity. Much of it is spent taking care of our basic needs and obligations, leaving precious few moments to indulge in other activities.
- **Time is continuous.** Time stops for no one. Whether we use it wisely or not, a day, an hour, a minute, or a second has passed, and there is no going back.

- **Time is limited.** Ever since sin entered this world our time has been confined to the space of a life span. None of us knows how long that life span will be. James compared our life to a mist that makes a brief appearance in the morning and then quickly vanishes (see James 4:14).

With these principles in mind, we then see the importance of wisely using our time and "making the most of every opportunity." Paul warned the church in Ephesus to be careful. We have to be careful because there are so many unimportant or trivial things that can crowd our time. We also must be careful of wasted time.

A study conducted in 2000 observed that the average American spends two days out of every week waiting in traffic, waiting in a line, waiting on the phone, or waiting on other people. Within this wasted time, we should look for opportunities. For example, if you find that you have little time for Bible reading or study during your day, would it be possible to listen to the Bible or sermon audio recordings during your work commute? As Christians, it should be our desire to direct people to Christ. If you spend time waiting in line or perhaps in a doctor's waiting room, do you attempt to connect with others waiting with you?

Paul counseled the church in Ephesus to live as wise instead of unwise persons. There is a difference between being smart and being wise. An individual can be very well educated in a scholarly sense and still be foolish. He/she may be highly intelligent, but not possess any wisdom. How so? Intelligence is the acquisition of knowledge. Wisdom is the ability to make practical use of knowledge. To develop wisdom, a Christian must commune with the source of wisdom—God. Proverbs 2:6 states, "For the LORD gives wisdom; from his mouth come knowledge and understanding." Bible study is paramount to obtaining wisdom needed to make the best use of opportunities presented (see also Psalm 111:10).

Paul reminded the early Christians that the "days are evil." All around them, the people of Ephesus were using their time to indulge in their own selfish pleasures. Paul cautioned against being sucked into time-consuming habits, for Christians are to make the most of every opportunity.

The message is relevant for Christians today. Although the world around us may seem to be living it up, they are only wasting it away. Wise persons understand that time is precious, limited, uncertain, and ongoing. Therefore, despite our other obligations, we make our service and worship a priority. We realize that in order to stand approved before the Lord we must constantly be renewed by keeping old bad habits at bay and replacing them with positive and godly qualities. We look for opportunities to improve ourselves and we seize them!

❖ Study Questions

1. What things should be of high priority in a Christian's life?

   _____
   _____
   _____

2. What key principles related to time do we do well to keep in mind?

   _____
   _____
   _____

3. Give examples of how you can make wiser use of your time.

   _____
   _____
   _____

4. What is wisdom?

   _____
   _____
   _____

5. How can a Christian gain wisdom? Read Psalm 111:10.

   _____

   _____

   _____

6. Understanding that time is precious, limited, uncertain, and ongoing, what should we be resolved to do?

   _____

   _____

   _____

www.ingramcontent.com/pod-product-compliance
Lightning Source LLC
Chambersburg PA
CBHW050508120526
44588CB00044B/1812